MUSIC THEORY IS FUN
Puzzles, Quizzes & Tests
Books 1 – 5 Answers

Maureen Cox

Canadian ISBN 978-1-987926-17-0

All enquiries regarding this paperback omnibus edition to:

Mimast Inc
email: mimast.inc@gmail.com

Comments on the original Theory is Fun books.

As a music teacher, I have all my children and adults start with this little book. The basics of music theory are laid out succinctly and clearly, with accompanying short exercises.

Dr T J Worrall

I'm a music teacher, and can honestly say this series of books is by far the most concise and fun to work with when helping kids. Adults also enjoy them.

C J Gascoine

Very thorough and approachable theory practice book for young students age 7 upwards.

Susan A. Harris

Theory can be a barrier for some young students but this book is set out well, it's easy to read and understand, and has logical progression. Highly recommended.

Steve Riches

I might at last be able to learn my theory and I am an old age pensioner learning to play the piano.

Violet

Very good book that puts things very simply. I was recommended this by my piano teacher even though I am an adult learner as it covers all the technical points very progressively.

Amazon Customer

Music Theory is Fun Book 1

978-1-987926-09-5

Treble clef, bass clef, notes and letter names. Time names and values. Dotted notes, tied notes and rests. Accidentals, tones and semitones. Key signatures and scales (C, G, D & F major). Degrees of the scale, intervals and tonic triads. Time signatures and bar-lines. Writing music and answering rhythms. Puzzles, quizzes and ten one-page tests. Musical terms dictionary and list of signs.

Music Theory is Fun Book 2

978-1-987926-10-1

Major key signatures to 3 sharps & flats. Minor keys to 1 sharp & flat. Degrees of the scale and intervals. Tonic triads. Keyboard, tones and semitones. Time signatures. Grouping notes and rests, triplets. Two ledger lines below and above the staves. Writing four-bar rhythms. Puzzles, quizzes and ten one-page tests. Musical terms and signs.

Music Theory is Fun Book 3

978-1-987926-11-8

Major & minor key signatures 4 sharps or flats. Harmonic and melodic minor scales. Degrees of the scale, intervals, tonic triads. Simple and compound time signatures. Grouping notes & rests. Transposition at the octave. More than two ledger lines. Writing four-bar rhythms, anacrusis. Phrases. Puzzles, quizzes and ten one-page tests. Musical terms & signs.

Music Theory is Fun Book 4

978-1-987926-12-5

Key signatures to 5 sharps or flats. Alto clef. Chromatic scale, double sharps & flats. Technical names of notes in the diatonic scale. Simple & compound time, duple, triple, quadruple. Primary triads, tonic, subdominant & dominant. Diatonic intervals up to an octave. Ornaments. Four-bar rhythms and rhythms to words. Orchestral instruments and their clefs. Puzzles, quizzes and ten one-page tests. Musical terms & signs including French.

Music Theory is Fun Book 5

978-1-987926-13-2

Key signatures to 7 sharps or flats. Tenor clef and scales. Compound intervals: major, minor, perfect, diminished & augmented. Irregular time signatures, quintuple & septuple. Tonic, super-tonic, subdominant & dominant chords. Writing at concert pitch. Short & open score. Orchestral instruments. Composing a melody. Perfect, imperfect & plagal cadences. Puzzles, quizzes and ten one-page tests. Musical terms and signs including French and German.

Music Theory is Fun – A Handy Reference

978-1-987926-14-9

A concise reference to all the rudiments of music covered by the above five Music Theory is Fun books.

If you want to play an instrument, sing well or just improve your listening, you need to read music and understand theory.

On your way through my five newly revised MUSIC THEORY IS FUN books you will find a variety of activities to help you along.

At the back of each book there are puzzles, quizzes and ten one-page tests composed of questions you could meet in an exam. Here in this book you will find the correct answers to those puzzles, quizzes and tests.

When a question could have more than one correct answer, you will find my answer inside a box like this:-

With my help you can enjoy mastering the theory of music and preparing for exams.

Maureen Cox

Acknowledgements

I am grateful to the many Professional Private Music Teachers and Members of the Incorporated Society of Musicians who used Theory is Fun with their pupils and to Christina Bourne, Brenda Harris, Alison Hogg, Judith Holmes, Ann Leggett and Marion Martin for their helpful suggestions. I am especially grateful to Alison Hounsome for her insightful comments and helpful recommendations in the preparation of this revised edition.

A word about Music Theory is Fun

Using the previous editions of my Theory is Fun, more than a half million people, young and not so young, mostly in the UK, had fun learning music theory. Music Theory is Fun is a revised edition designed to include students in America, Canada and other countries where, for example, a bar is a measure, a minim is a half note and a tone is a whole step. Common alternatives terms and a full dictionary of musical terms and signs are also listed at the back of each book.

My Music Theory is Fun books have been extended to include a variety of puzzles, quizzes and tests to cover the basic rudiments of theory required by the various Boards and Colleges including the Associated Board of the Royal Schools of Music, Trinity College London, the Music Examinations Boards of Australia and New Zealand and the Royal Conservatory of Canada.

Any errors are entirely my responsibility. Should there be any in this edition, I would be most grateful for them to be drawn to my attention so that they may be corrected in a future edition.

Maureen Cox

BOOK 1
PUZZLES

QUIZZES

TESTS

Fun page

Connect the note to the rest of the same length.

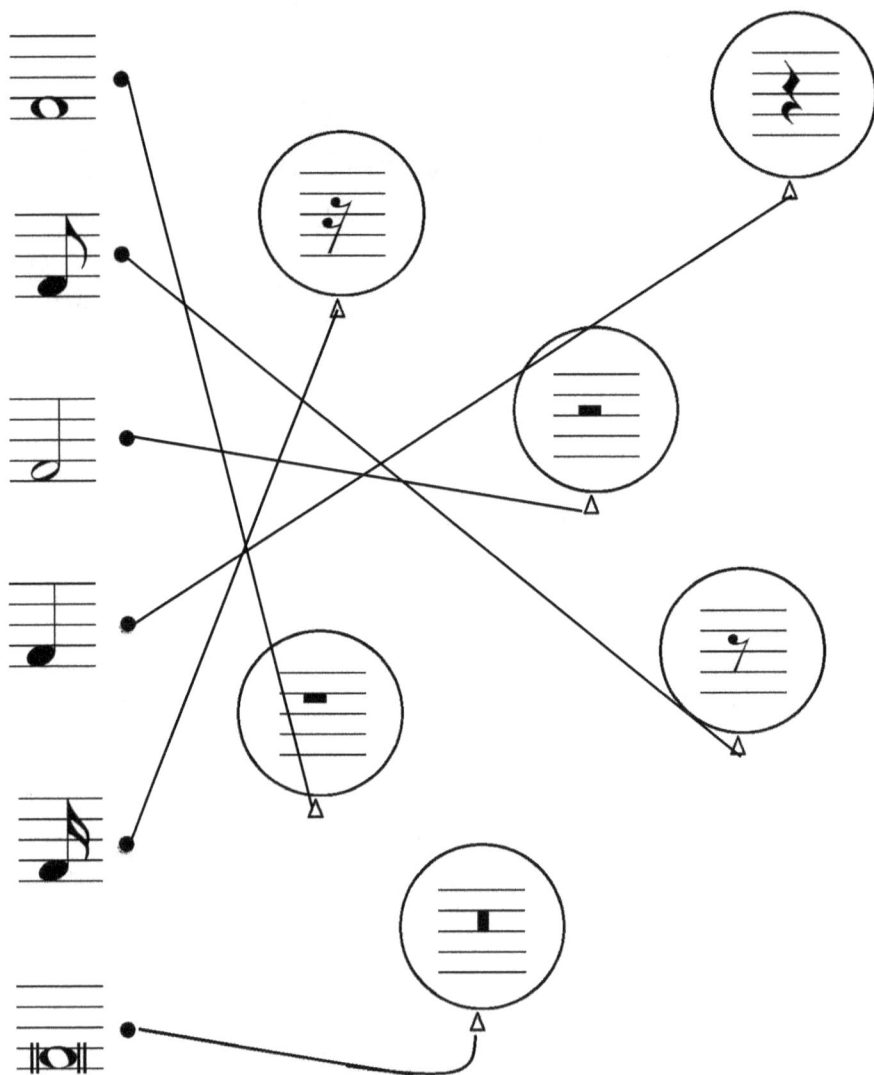

I connected the longest note and rest.
You will meet them in Book 3.

Merry-go-round

The last letter or the last two letters of one word will be the start of the next word. Go around the shell to find the answers to the questions below.

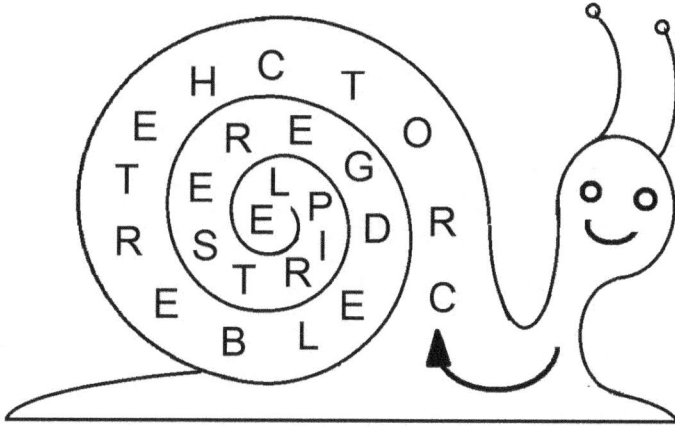

This is a **CROTCHET** / *quarter note*.

This is the called the **TREBLE** clef.

These notes are on **LEDGER** lines.

This is called a **REST**.

This is indicates simple **TRIPLE** time.

Word search

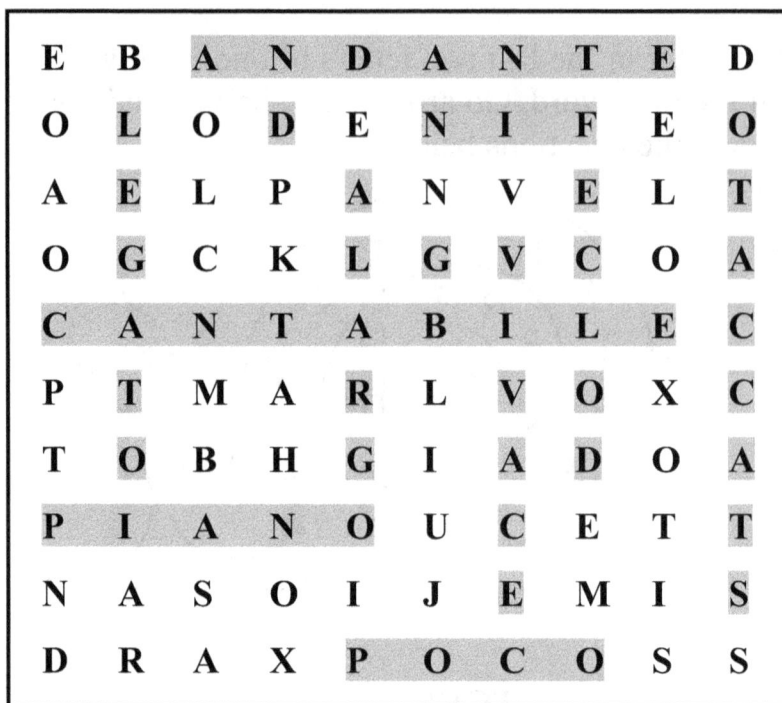

E	B	A	N	D	A	N	T	E	D
O	L	O	D	E	N	I	F	E	O
A	E	L	P	A	N	V	E	L	T
O	G	C	K	L	G	V	C	O	A
C	A	N	T	A	B	I	L	E	C
P	T	M	A	R	L	V	O	X	C
T	O	B	H	G	I	A	D	O	A
P	I	A	N	O	U	C	E	T	T
N	A	S	O	I	J	E	M	I	S
D	R	A	X	P	O	C	O	S	S

Meaning	Musical term
A little	**poco**
At a walking pace	**andante**
Slow, stately, broad	**largo**
Soft	**piano**
The end	**fin**
Smoothly	**legato**
In a singing style	**cantabile**
Slow, leisurely	**adagio**
Lively, quick	**vivace**
Sweetly	**dolce**
Short, detached	**staccato**

Crossword

Clues

Across

1 gradually slower
4 loud
6 3rd and 4th degree of C major
7 speed, time
10 slow and stately, broad
11 6th and 7th degrees of D major
12 sweetly
13 gradually softer

Down

1 becoming gradually slower
2 slow, leisurely
3 gradually softer
5 tonic triad
8 1st, 2nd and 3rd degrees in the scale of F major
9 lively, quick

Quiz 1

Put a tick / *check mark* (✔) in the correct box.

1. adagio

☐ at a walking pace

☑ slow, leisurely

☐ lively, reasonably fast

☐ slightly slower than allegro

2. staccato

☐ suddenly

☐ smoothly

☐ very quick

☑ short, detached

3. sweetly

☐ cantabile

☑ dolce

☐ maestoso

☐ pesante

4. quietly

☐ forte

☐ leggiero

☑ piano

☐ tranquillo

5. scherzo

☑ a joke

☐ lightly

☐ heavily

☐ playfully

6. gradually softer

☑ decresc.

☐ rall.

☐ rit.

☐ *sfz*

Quiz 2

Put a tick / *check mark* (✔) in the correct box.

1. $\diagdown$

- ☐ becoming louder
- ☑ becoming softer
- ☐ accent the note
- ☐ slur

2. $>$

- ☐ becoming softer
- ☑ accent the note
- ☐ pause on the note
- ☐ short, detached

3. $\diagup$

- ☐ becoming softer
- ☑ becoming louder
- ☐ becoming slower
- ☐ short, detached

4. ⌢ ⌣

- ☐ short, detached
- ☐ accent the note
- ☐ play an octave higher
- ☑ pause on the note

5. **play notes smoothly**

- ☐ 8va / 8
- ☐ ◁▷
- ☑ ⌒
- ☐ ⌢ ⌣

6. **gradually louder**

- ☐ *sfz*
- ☑ **cresc.**
- ☐ **rall.**
- ☐ **rit**

Handy hints for tests

This section is for you to practise the different types of questions you could have in a test or an exam.

The questions could be on any topic covered in this book.

Revise each topic in this book thoroughly.

Don't forget to study musical terms and signs – they are **always** included.

Practice
makes perfect !

Practice
makes perfect !

If you have worked through this book carefully and understood each topic, this will be an easy task for you.

Before you begin any test, write out your key signature chart from page 39. Always refer to the chart when tackling questions that require you to know a key signature.

Test 1

Put a tick / *check mark* (✓) in the correct box.

1. Name this note:

      A ☐   D ☑   B ☐

2. Name this note:

      B natural ☐   G flat ☐   B flat ☑

3. Name the notes to find the hidden word:

      CAFE ☑   CAGE ☐   FACE ☐

4. How many quavers / *eighth notes* are there in a minim / *half note*?

   2 ☐   4 ☑   8 ☐

5. For how many crotchets / *quarter notes* does this rest last?

      3 ☐   2 ☑   4 ☐

6. Which is the correct time signature?

    $\frac{3}{4}$ ☐ $\frac{4}{4}$ ☑ $\frac{2}{4}$ ☐

Test 2

1. Which pair of notes has a distance / *step* of a semitone / *half step* between them?

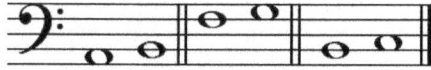

    A and B ☐   F and G ☐   B and C ☑

2. Here is the scale of F major. Where are the semitones / *half steps*?

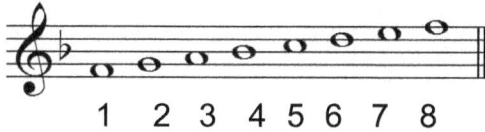

    1 2 3 4 5 6 7 8

Between 1st and 2nd and 7th and 8th degrees ☐
Between 3rd and 4th and 7th and 8th degrees ☑
Between 5th and 6th and 7th and 8th degrees ☐

3. Which is the correct key signature of D major?

 ☐   ☑   ☐

4. Choose the key note for this tonic triad.

    F ☑   G ☐   C ☐

5. Which note needs to be added to complete this tonic triad in G major?

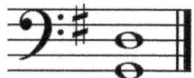

    C ☐   B ☑   A ☐

6. Name this interval.

    5th ☐   7th ☐   6th ☑

Test 3

Write the words.

1.
A   C   E

2.
C   A   G   E

3.
B   E   E

4.
D   E   A   F

5.
A   D   D

6.
F   E   E   D

7.
B   E   D

8.
F   A   C   E

9.
E   G   G

10.
E   D   G   E

11.
F   A   D

12.
B   E   E   F

Test 4

Write the notes.

1. B E G

2. B A D

3. F A D E D

4. C A B B A G E

5. A D D   C A F E

7. B E G G E D

8. B A G G A G E

Test 5

1. 2 crotchets / *2 quarter notes* = 1 **minim** / *1 half note*

2. *2 semiquavers* / *2 sixteenth notes* = 1 **quaver** / *1 quarter note*

3. 2 quavers / *2 eighth notes* = 1 **crotchet** / *1 quarter note*

4. 1 minim / *1 half note* = **4 quavers** / *4 quarter notes*.

5. 1 semibreve / *1 whole note* = **2 minims** / *2 half notes*.

6. 1 crotchet / *1 quarter note* = **4 semiquavers** / *4 8th notes*.

7. In $\frac{4}{4}$ time you can beam together beats **1 & 2** and **3 & 4**.

8. In $\frac{4}{4}$ time you cannot beam together beats **2** and **3**.

9. $\frac{3}{4}$ is simple **triple** time.

10. $\frac{2}{4}$ is simple **duple** time.

11. Write a whole bar of quavers / *eighth notes*.

12. Write a whole bar of quavers / *eighth notes*.

Test 6

1. Write the scale of F major going up, one octave only. Use semibreves / *whole notes*. Put in the key signature. Mark the semitones / *half steps* with a bracket ⌐¬ or ⌐_⌐.

2. There are mistakes in the following music. Write it out correctly.

3. Answer the following rhythm.

4. Name the notes in the tonic triad of G major.

GBD ☑   GBC ☐   GAD ☐

5. Name these intervals.

(a) **6th**   (b) **3rd**   (c) **5th**

(d) **4th**   (e) **7th**   (f) **2nd**

Test 7

1. Write a higher note above each given note to make the named harmonic interval. The first one has been done for you. The key is C major.

(a) 5th

(b) 3rd

(c) 6th

(d) 4th

(e) 7th

(f) 8th/8ve

2. Name the key of each scale. Draw a bracket over the notes that make a semitone / *half step*. The first one is done for you.

(a) C major

(b) G major

(c) D major

(d) F major

Test 8

1. Name the degree of the scale of the notes marked * . The key is C major.

5th   2nd   7th   4th   6th   8th

2. Name the key of each tonic triad.

C major   F major   G major   D major

3. Write tonic triads with key signature for the following:

F major   G major   D major

4. Write these dynamics in the correct order from the quietest to the loudest.

f   *mp*   *ff*   *pp*   *mf*   *p*

pp   *p*   *mp*   *mf*   *f*   *ff*

5. Name the key of this scale **F major**
   and mark the semitones / *half steps* with   .

Test 9

Answer the questions on these eight bars / *measures*.

1. What is the major key of this music?

   F major

2. How many crotchets / *quarter notes* are in a bar / *measure*?

   4 (four)

3. In which bar / *measure* is the rhythm the same as bar / *measure* 5?

   bar / *measure* 7

4. Write the meaning of

   Presto **very quick**
   mf **moderately loud**

5. Which bars /*measures* have only staccato notes?

   bars / *measures* 1 and 6

6. Write the highest and lowest notes as crotchets / *quarter notes*.

Test 10

1. Copy the piece of music above. Include the clef, key signature, time signature and all other details shown.

   In this F major melody

2. What is the letter name of the highest note? **F**

3. Name the degree of the scale in bar 2. **1st**

4. Which bar / *measure* has all the notes of the tonic triad? **3**

5. How many staccato notes are there? **4 (four)**

6. Answer true or false to this statement.
   The notes in bar / *measure* 5 are the quietest. **false**

7. Write the meaning of

   pp   **very soft**

    becoming louder

8. What is the meaning of Andante?

   at a walking pace

9. Which bar / *measure* has a dotted crotchet / *dotted quarter note*? **3**

MIM

BOOK 2
PUZZLES

QUIZZES

TESTS

Fun page

Draw a string for each balloon. I drew the first for you.

3 crotchets / *3 quarter beats* in a bar -

4 minims / *4 half beats* in a bar -

3 quavers / *3 eighth beats* in a bar -

2 minims / *2 half beats* in a bar -

4 crotchets / *4 quarter beats* in a bar -

3 minims / *3 half beats* in a bar

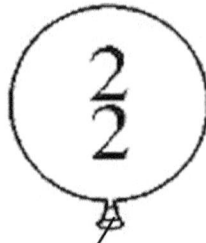

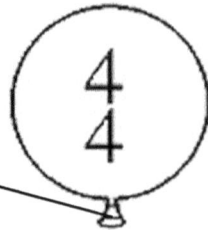

$\dfrac{2}{2}$

$\dfrac{3}{8}$

$\dfrac{3}{4}$

$\dfrac{4}{2}$

$\dfrac{3}{2}$

$\dfrac{4}{4}$

Musical matchword

Can you join the boxes to make ten musical words?   I have joined the first one for you.

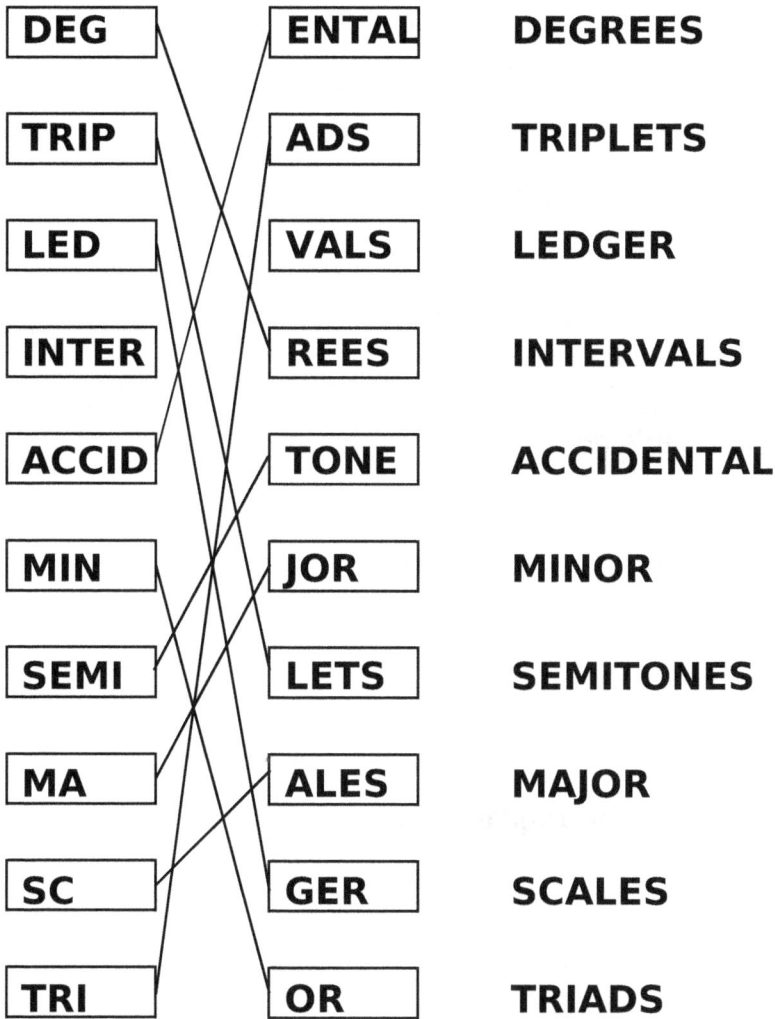

DEG	ENTAL	DEGREES
TRIP	ADS	TRIPLETS
LED	VALS	LEDGER
INTER	REES	INTERVALS
ACCID	TONE	ACCIDENTAL
MIN	JOR	MINOR
SEMI	LETS	SEMITONES
MA	ALES	MAJOR
SC	GER	SCALES
TRI	OR	TRIADS

Musical Anagrams

techcrot / *traquer eton*   **crotchet** / *quarter note*

Clue: A note worth four semiquavers / *4 sixteenth notes*.

dregle sinle   **ledger lines**

Clue: These are above and below the stave.

charmion   **harmonic**

Clue: For this interval play the notes together.

comidel   **melodic**

Clue: For this interval play the notes separately.

veremibes / *weloh tone*   **semibreve** / *whole note*

Clue: A whole bar's rest hangs from the line.

vertinal   **interval**

Clue: Count from the keynote to find its number.

icont dratis   **tonic triads**

Clue: These use the 1st, 3rd and 5th notes of a scale.

plaquedur   **quadruple**

Clue: The time with four beats in a bar.

pliter   **triple**

Clue: The time with three beats in a bar.

pudle   **duple**

Clue: The time with two beats in a bar.

Crossword

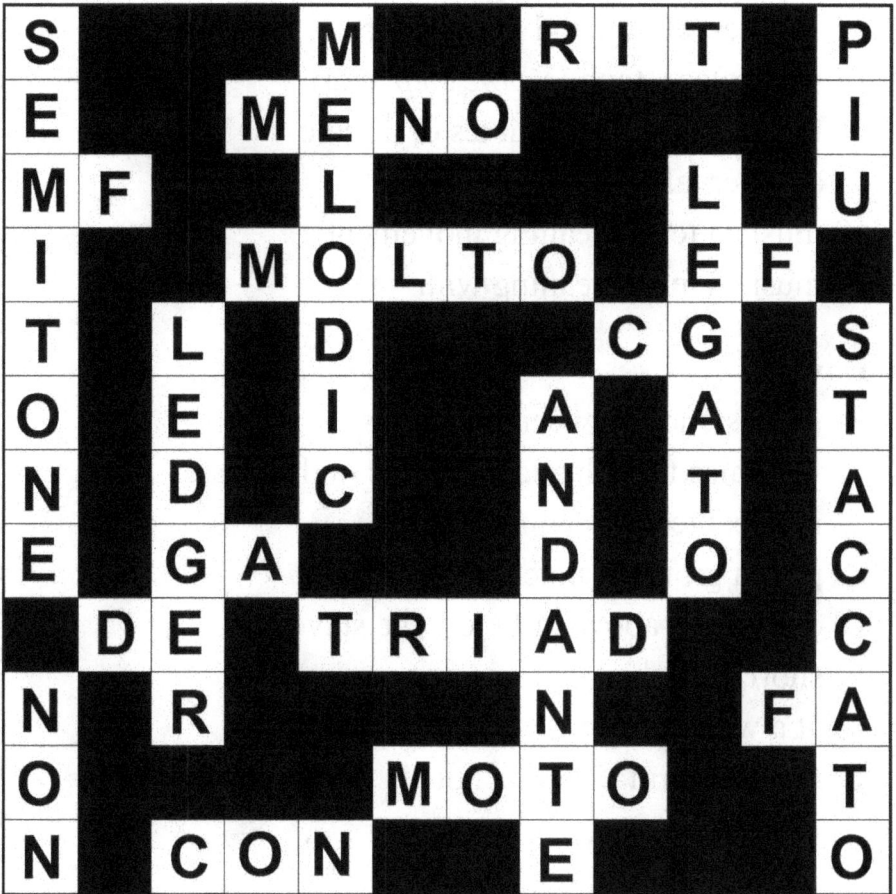

Clues

Across

3 hold back, slower at once

5 musical term meaning less

6 short for moderately loud

8 musical term meaning much

9 two notes a semitone / *half step* apart

11 an interval of a 5th in C major

14 an interval of a 2nd in G major

15 two notes a tone / *whole step* apart

16 the 1st, 3rd and 5th notes of a scale

18 an interval of a 3rd in F major

19 musical term meaning movement

20 musical term meaning with

Down

1 the distance between two notes

2 you raise the 6th and 7th notes in this scale

4 musical term meaning more

7 play a group of notes smoothly

10 extra lines above or below the stave

12 short, detached

13 at a walking pace

17 musical term meaning not

Musical terms word search

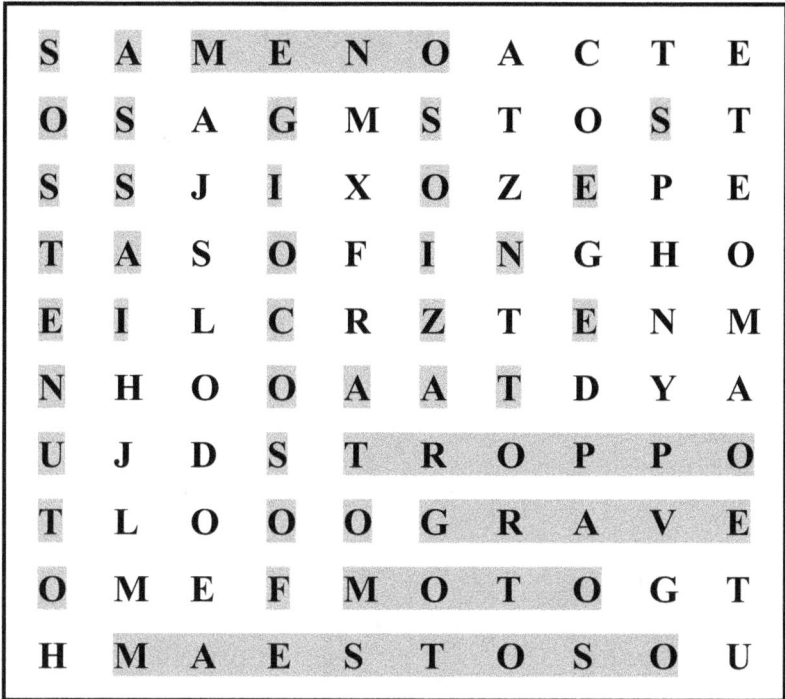

S	A	M	E	N	O	A	C	T	E
O	S	A	G	M	S	T	O	S	T
S	S	J	I	X	O	Z	E	P	E
T	A	S	O	F	I	N	G	H	O
E	I	L	C	R	Z	T	E	N	M
N	H	O	O	A	A	T	D	Y	A
U	J	D	S	T	R	O	P	P	O
T	L	O	O	G	R	A	V	E
O	M	E	F	M	O	T	O	G	T
H	M	A	E	S	T	O	S	O	U

Meaning	Musical term
movement	**moto**
majestically	**maestoso**
gracefully	**grazioso**
sustained	**sostenuto**
very slow	**grave**
too much	**troppo**
without	**senza**
less	**meno**
merry	**giocoso**
loud	**forte**
very	**assai**

Quiz 1

Put a tick / *check mark* (✔) in the correct box.

1. allargando

☐ at a walking pace

☐ slow, leisurely

☑ broadening out

☐ very quick

2. larghetto

☑ faster than largo

☐ slow and stately

☐ very slow

☐ at a walking pace

3. sustained

☐ subito

☑ sostenuto

☐ maestoso

☐ ritenuto

4. held on

☐ marcato

☐ staccato

☐ subito

☑ tenuto

5. mosso

☐ less

☐ more

☑ movement

☐ much

6. semi-staccato

☐

☐

☐

☑

Quiz 2

True (**T**) or False (**F**)?

1. The key of C major has no sharps or flats. **T** ☑ **F** ☐

2. The key of B♭ major has two flats. **T** ☑ **F** ☐

3. The key of A major has three sharps. **T** ☑ **F** ☐

4. The key of E minor has three flats. **T** ☐ **F** ☑

5. The 7th note in a harmonic minor scale is raised one semitone / *one half step* ascending and descending. **T** ☑ **F** ☐

6. In E♭ major the 6th degree is B♭. **T** ☐ **F** ☑

7. The two notes in a melodic interval are written one above the other and played at the same time. **T** ☐ **F** ☑

8. The tonic triad of D minor is D F♯ A. **T** ☐ **F** ☑

9. The symbol ₵ means two minim / *2 half note* beats in the bar. **T** ☑ **F** ☐

10. A minim rest / *half note* is used for a whole bar's rest in $\frac{4}{4}$ time. **T** ☐ **F** ☑

Handy hints for tests

This section is for you to practise the different types of questions you could have in a test or an exam.

The questions could be on any topic covered in this book and in Music Theory is Fun Book 1.

Revise each topic in this book thoroughly.

Don't forget to study musical terms and signs – they are **always** included.

Practice
makes perfect !

Practice
makes perfect !

If you have worked through this book carefully and understood each topic, this will be an easy task for you.

Before you begin any test, write out your key signature chart from memory (see page 22). Always refer to the chart when tackling questions that require you to know a key signature.

Test 1

Put a tick / *check mark* (✓) in the box next to the correct answer.

1. Name this note:

   C sharp ☑   A sharp ☐   G natural ☐

2. How many crotchet / *quarter note* beats are in a bar with this time signature?

   2 ☐   3 ☐   4 ☑

3. For how many quaver / *eighth note* beats does this rest last?

   2 ☑   3 ☐   4 ☐

4. Add the total number of crotchet / *quarter note* beats of silence in these rests.

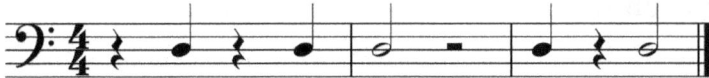

   6 ☐   5 ☑   4 ☐

5. The relative minor of F major is:

   D minor ☑   A minor ☐   E minor ☐

6. Name this scale.

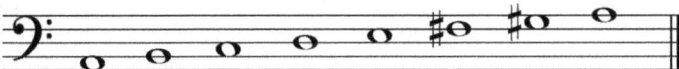

   G melodic minor ☐
   A melodic minor ☑
   E harmonic minor ☐

Test 2

1. Write a triplet of 3 quavers / *3 eighth notes* or
   3 semiquavers / *3 sixteenth notes* where you see *.

(a)

(b)

(c)

2. Name the key of this tonic triad.

   D major

3. Complete each line to make a 4-bar rhythm.

(a)

(b)

(c)

(d)

Test 3

1. Write a one-octave E♭ major scale with key signature in semibreves / *whole notes* descending.
   Mark the semitones / *half steps*.

2. Write a one-octave A major scale without key signature in crotchets / *quarter notes* ascending. Put in accidentals where needed and mark the semitones / *half steps*.

3. Write a one-octave E harmonic minor scale without key signature in minims / *half notes* descending. Put in accidentals where needed and mark the semitones / *half steps*.

4. Write a one-octave D melodic minor scale with key signature in crotchets / *quarter notes* ascending.
   Mark the semitones / *half steps*.

Book 2 page 54

Test 4

1. Here are four pieces of music. Add a time signature to each of them.

(a)

(b)

(c)

(d)

2. Write a higher note above each given note to make the named harmonic interval.

(a)
4th

(b)
3rd

(c)
8th

(d)
7th

(e)
5th

(f)
6th

3. Add the clef and any sharps or flats for this E♭ major scale.

Test 5

1. Write the letter names for each of the notes marked *.
   Include the sharp or flat.

C#   E   D   A   F#   B

2. Write the notes in the correct order of the time values
   beginning with the longest and ending with the shortest.

3. Name the keys of these tonic triads.

(a) C major   (b) Bb major   (c) E minor

(d) Eb major   (e) D major

4. Write this passage of music in notes and rests of twice the
   value.

Book 2 page 56

Test 6

Look at this passage of music then answer the questions.

1. Name the key of this piece.
   D minor

2. What type of beat is shown in the time signature?
   quaver or eighth note

3. How many beats are there in each bar / *measure*? **3**

4. What is the meaning of presto? **very quick**

5. How should you play the two notes in bar 2?
   slowly ☐   smoothly ☑   quickly ☐

6. How many bars have staccato notes?
   6 ☐   5 ☐   4 ☑

7. How many accented notes are there in this piece?
   6 ☐   4 ☐   3 ☑

8. What does *ff* mean? **very loud**

Test 7

Look at this melody then answer the questions below.

1. Copy the music from bar 5 to the end just as it is written.

2. Name the first four notes in bar 6.

   (a) **F**   (b) **D**   (c) **C**   (d) **B♭**

3. Which two bars have the same rhythms? **bars 5 and 6**

4. What is the meaning of allegro? **lively, reasonably fast**

5. Write the letter name of the highest note. **F**

6. How should the first two notes be played? **short, detached**

7. What does ⌢ mean over the note in bar 4?
   pause on the note

8. Which bar has the note with the strongest accent? **bar 8**

9. Name the degree of the scale (e.g. 1st, 2nd) of the first
   note in bar 3. **6th (sixth)**

Test 8

1. This passage of music has no time signature. Work out what it should be and write it in the correct place.

2. Copy out bars 1-4 in the treble clef without a key signature. Remember to write an accidental if needed and to put in the time signature. Write neatly and accurately.

3. Name the major key of the melody. **G major**

4. Name the minor key with the same key signature. **E minor**

5. Name the notes in bar 7. **G F♯ G**

6. Name the interval (number only) between notes 2 and 3 of bar 2. **3rd**

7. Which bar has the same rhythm as bar 3? **bar 2**

8. Circle the note worth 3 crotchets / *3 quarter notes* in the passage.

9. Circle two notes next to each other which make an octave interval.

Test 9

Look at this melody and answer the questions below.

1. Find a triplet in the passage and copy it here.

2. Find in the passage two notes next to each other and a semitone / *a half step* apart. Copy them here.

3. Raise each note in bar 1 a semitone / *a half step* and write them here.

4. Lower each note in bar 5 a semitone / *a half step* and write them here.

5. Copy out bar 4 in the bass clef and put in the key signature.

6. Give the meaning of the following:

repeat

mf **moderately loud**

lento **slowly**

crotchet / *quarter note* rest

Test 10

1. This passage of music has no time signature. Work out what it should be and write it in the correct place.

2. Write the notes in bar 4 one octave lower in the bass clef. Put in the key signature.

3. How many staccato notes are there?   **14**

4. Name the intervals in bar 10 between

   (a) notes 1 and 2   **2nd**

   (b) notes 2 and 3   **4th**

5. Give the meaning of

   sfz   **with a sudden accent**

   mp   **moderately soft**

      becoming louder

   Andante   **at a walking pace**

   >   **accent note**

   f   **loud**

BOOK 3
PUZZLES

QUIZZES

TESTS

Crossword

Clues

Across

1 dying away

2 1st, 2nd and 3rd degrees of G major

4 interval of a perfect 8th (an octave)
in C Major, beginning on the tonic

6 from

11interval of a 4th in E major, starting on the keynote

12 interval of a 4th in G minor, starting on the keynote

14 with

15 interval of a 6th in D major, starting on the keynote

16 tonic triad of A minor

17 sadly

Down

1 movement

3 with boldness and spirit

5 in a singing style

8 fire

9 sign

10 go on immediately

13 the end

Musical Matchword

Can you join the boxes to make ten musical words?   I have joined the first one for you.

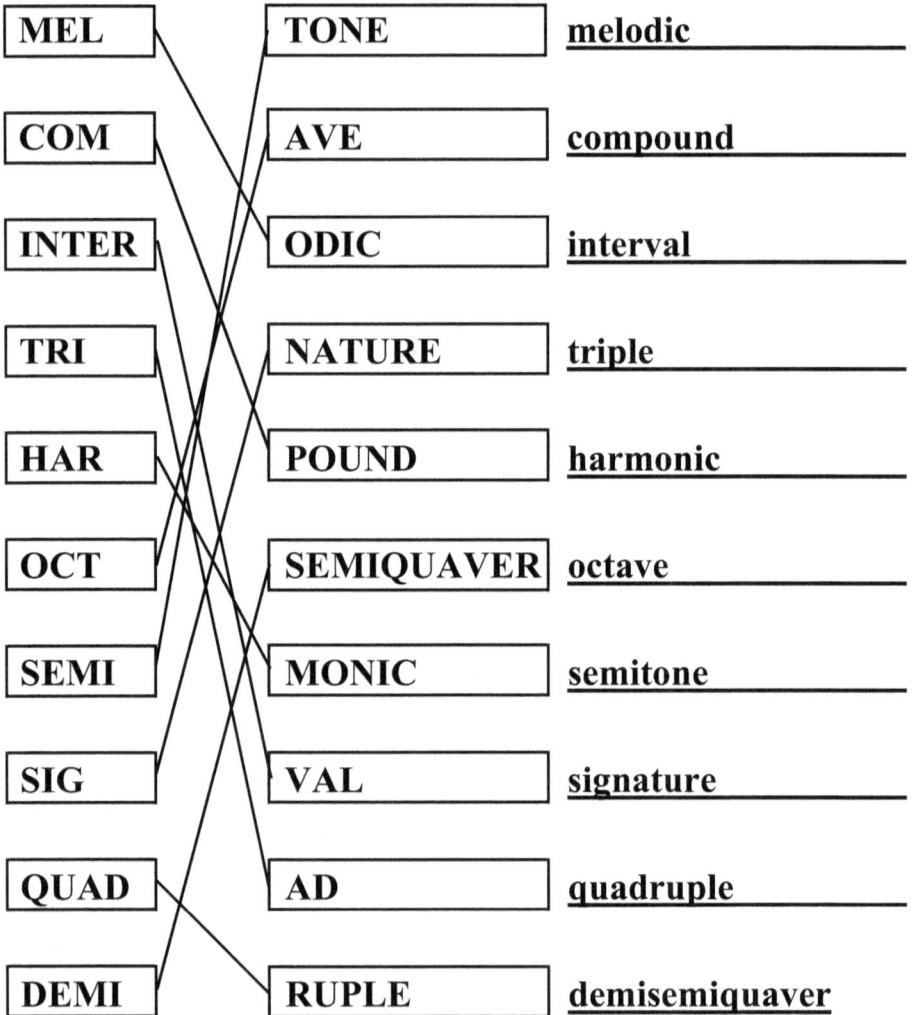

MEL	TONE	melodic
COM	AVE	compound
INTER	ODIC	interval
TRI	NATURE	triple
HAR	POUND	harmonic
OCT	SEMIQUAVER	octave
SEMI	MONIC	semitone
SIG	VAL	signature
QUAD	AD	quadruple
DEMI	RUPLE	demisemiquaver

Musical Anagrams

noisetem / *lafh pest* | **semitone / *whole step***

Clue: The interval between notes 2&3 in a minor scale.

charmion | **harmonic**

Clue: You raise the 7th note one semitone / *half step* ascending and descending in this minor scale.

domicel | **melodic**

Clue: The interval between notes 5&6 is one semitone / *half step* when descending this minor scale.

citon driat | **tonic triad**

Clue: The 1st, 3rd and 5th notes of a scale.

trivalen | **interval**

Clue: Always count both notes when working out one of these.

calendatics | **accidentals**

Clue: Sharps, flats and naturals.

Musical Boxes

Use these letters to complete the words in the musical boxes.

B E E H I I J L L M O P P Q R T

MA _J_ OR

_M_ IN _O_ R

TREB _L_ _E_

_B_ ASS

MIN _I_ M

CRO _T_ C _H_ ET

SEM _I_ BR _E_ VE

DU _P_ LE

TRIP _L_ E

_Q_ UAD _R_ U _P_ LE

Musical terms word search

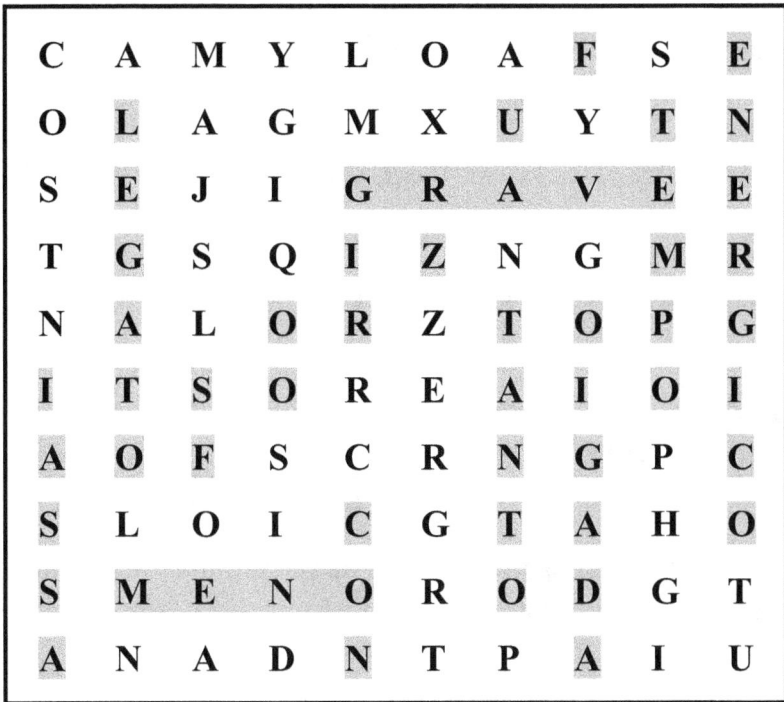

C	A	M	Y	L	O	A	F	S	E
O	L	A	G	M	X	U	Y	T	N
S	E	J	I	G	R	A	V	E	E
T	G	S	Q	I	Z	N	G	M	R
N	A	L	O	R	Z	T	O	P	G
I	T	S	O	R	E	A	I	O	I
A	O	F	S	C	R	N	G	P	C
S	L	O	I	C	G	T	A	H	O
S	M	E	N	O	R	O	D	G	T
A	N	A	D	N	T	P	A	I	U

Meaning	Musical term
less	**meno**
force, power	**forza**
with energy	**energico**
furiously	**furioso**
smoothly	**legato**
slow, leisurely	**adagio**
with	**con**
very slow	**grave**
speed, time	**tempo**
so much	**tanto**
very	**assai**

Quiz 1

1. How many sharps are in the E major key signature?

    1 ☐   2 ☐   3 ☐   4 ☑   5 ☐

2. How many flats are in the E♭ major key signature?

    1 ☐   2 ☐   3 ☑   4 ☐   5 ☐

3. How many sharps are in the C♯ minor key signature?

    1 ☐   2 ☐   3 ☐   4 ☑   5 ☐

4. How many demisemiquavers / *32nd notes* are in a crotchet / *quarter note*?

    2 ☐   4 ☐   6 ☐   7 ☐   8 ☑

5. Which notes in a melodic minor scale are raised one semitone when ascending and lowered when descending?

    3 and 4 ☐   5 and 6 ☐   6 and 7 ☑

6. Which beats can you not beam together in 4/4 time?

    1 and 2 ☐   2 and 3 ☑   3 and 4 ☐

7. Which time signature is a simple triple time?

    $\frac{3}{8}$ ☑ $\frac{6}{8}$ ☐ $\frac{9}{8}$ ☐

8. Which time signature is a compound quadruple time?

    $\frac{4}{2}$ ☐ $\frac{4}{4}$ ☐ $\frac{12}{8}$ ☑

9. Which rest is used for a whole bar in $\frac{4}{2}$ time?

    ☑   ☐   ☐

10. Which rest is used for a whole bar in $\frac{3}{4}$ time?

    ☐   ☑   ☐

Book 3 page 48

Quiz 2

Put a tick / *check mark* (✓) in the correct box.

1. adagietto

☐ at a walking pace

☑ rather slow

☐ slightly slower than allegro

☐ slow, leisurely

2. largamente

☑ in a broad style

☐ slow and stately

☐ very slow

☐ sad, sorrowful

3. gradually faster

☐ slentando

☐ sostenuto

☑ stringendo

☐ subito

4. grief, sorrow

☐ dolce

☐ dolente

☑ dolore

☐ lacrimoso

5. mesto

☐ less

☐ more

☐ much

☑ sadly

6. quaver / *8th note* rest

☐

☐

☐

☑

Book 3 page 49

Quiz 3

1. **morendo** means

   dying away ☑   simple ☐

   sad, sorrowful ☐   too much ☐

2. **scherzando** means

   majestically ☐   playfully ☑

   gracefully ☐   with feeling ☐

3. **sospirando** means

   softly ☐   sustained ☐

   sad, sorrowful ☐   sighing ☑

4. **vivace** means

   lively, quick ☑   vibrating ☐

   with feeling ☐   boldly ☐

5. **tempo rubato** means

   with some freedom of time ☑

   at a comfortable speed ☐

   resume the original speed ☐

   gradually faster ☐

6. *fp* means

   loud then gradually softer ☐

   with a strong accent ☐

   loud then immediately soft ☑

   furiously ☐

Handy hints for tests

This section is for you to practise the different types of questions you could have in a test or an exam.

The questions could be on any topic covered in this book and in Music Theory is Fun Books 1 and 2.

Revise each topic in this book thoroughly.

Don't forget to study musical terms and signs – they are **always** included.

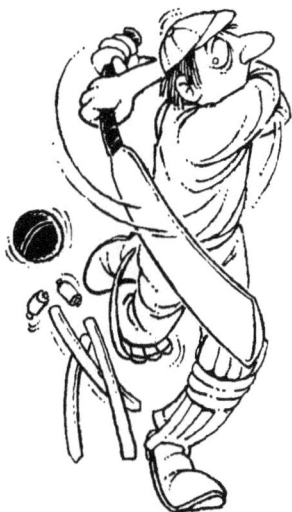

Practice
makes perfect !

Practice
makes perfect !

If you have worked through this book carefully and understood each topic, this will be an easy task for you.

Before you begin any test, write out your key signature chart (see page 15). Always refer to the chart when tackling questions that require you to know a key signature.

Test 1

Put a tick / *check mark* (✓) in the box next to the correct answer.

1. Name this note:

   C ☐   B♭ ☐   F ☑

2. How many beats of silence are in these bars?

   3 ☐   4 ☑   5 ☐

3. Which is the correct time signature?

   $\frac{3}{4}$ ☐ $\frac{6}{8}$ ☑ $\frac{3}{2}$ ☐

4. Which time signature is in simple time?

   C ☑ $\frac{9}{8}$ ☐ $\frac{6}{8}$ ☐

5. The relative major of C minor is:

   B♭ major ☐   A♭ major ☐   E♭ major ☑

6. The major scale with a key signature of three sharps is:

   D major ☐   A major ☑   E major ☐

7. Which degrees of the scale do you change to form melodic minor scales when ascending?

   5th & 6th ☐   5th & 7th ☐   6th & 7th ☑

8. Name this interval.

   perfect 5th ☐   major 6th ☑   major 7th ☐

Book 3 page 52

Test 2

1. = one **dotted quaver** / *dotted eighth note*

2. = one **crotchet** / *quarter note*

3. **32** demisemiquavers / *32nd notes* = one semibreve / *whole note*

4. = **3** minims / *half notes*

5. A semibreve / *whole note* = **8** quavers / *8th notes*

6. Choose from the words simple, compound, duple, triple and quadruple to describe the following time signatures.

   $\frac{4}{4}$ **simple quadruple time**

   $\frac{9}{8}$ **compound triple time**

7. When a rhythm begins before the first beat of a bar 1, this is called an **anacrusis**.

8. When you write the final bar, you must subtract the value of the **anacrusis**.

9. Write a 2 bar rhythm to follow each anacrusis.

Book 3 page 53

Test 3

1. Name this triad.

 F♯ minor ☑   F minor ☐   A major ☐

2. Name this minor key signature.

 D minor ☐   C♯ minor ☑   E minor ☐

3. Write a one-octave G harmonic minor scale in minims / *half notes*, ascending in the treble clef, without key signature. Remember the accidentals.

4. Write a one-octave C melodic minor scale in crotchets / *quarter notes*, descending in the bass clef, with key signature.

5. There are mistakes in this piece of music. Rewrite it correcting them.

Adanteo

mf

Andante

mf

Test 4

1. Write a whole bar of quavers / *eighth notes* in the bottom space in each of these times shown.

(a)

(b)

(c)

2. Write a whole bar of semiquavers / *sixteenth notes* in the top space in each of these times shown.

(a)

(b)

(c)

Test 5

1. Add the missing bar lines to each of these melodies, all of which begin on the first beat.

2. Add the correct clef and any necessary sharp or flat signs to complete each of these scales. Do not use key signatures.

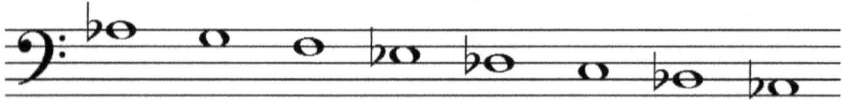

A flat major

F sharp harmonic minor

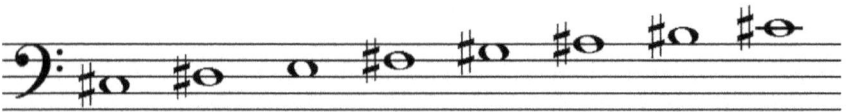

C sharp melodic minor

3. Write the letter name of each note on the lines below.

C♯   A♭   A♯   B♭   E

Test 6

1. Name each of these intervals as shown in the first answer.

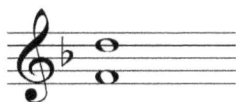   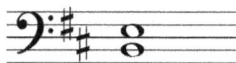   

   major 6th   **perfect 4th**   **major 7th**

      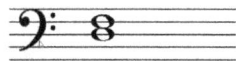

   perfect 5th   **octave/perfect 8th**   **minor 3rd**

2. Add the correct rest(s) where you see * to make each bar complete.

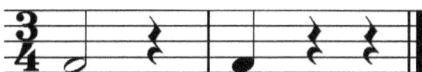   

3. Rewrite this music with the notes correctly beamed.

4. Write the key signature and tonic triad in semibreves / *whole notes* for each of the following keys.

   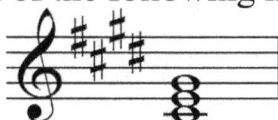   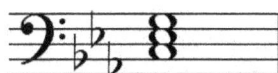

   A major   C♯ minor   C minor

Book 3 page 57

Test 7

1. Write these notes an octave higher in the treble clef.

2. Write the key signature and tonic triad in semibreves / *whole notes* for each of the following keys.

(a) F minor

(b) B♭ major

(c) F♯ minor

(d) A♭ major

3. Write in semibreves / *whole notes* the scale of B melodic minor ascending and descending without key signature.

4. Write one bar of rhythm in each of the following compound times. Use the note G.

Book 3 page 58

Test 8

Look at these four bars then answer the questions below.

1. Using the blank stave above, write out bars 3 and 4 an octave lower in the bass clef.

2. Name the key of this piece.   **D minor**

3. The time signature tells you that

   (a) there should be **2** beats in a bar and

   (b) that they are **crotchet / *quarter note*** beats.

4. Name the semiquavers / *16th notes* in bar 3.

   A   B flat   C sharp   D

5. Give the number of the bar that contains all the notes of the tonic triad. **bar 1**

6. Give the meaning of presto: **very quick**

7. How should you play the last note?

   strongly accented

8. How should the first four notes in bar 1 be played?

   staccato / detached

9. How should the first four notes in bar 3 be played?

   staccato/detached and becoming louder

Book 3 page 59

Test 9

Look at the following piece then answer the questions below.

1. Using the blank stave below, write out bars 5 and 6 an octave lower and in the bass clef.

2. What does 𝄿 mean at the end of bar 8?
   end the repeat of the passage

3. In bar 3 how should you play notes 4 and 5 joined by ⌣ ?
   tie together

4. What does **C** mean?
   2 minim / *half note* beats in a bar

5. What is the loudest note in the piece? Name the note and bar number.
   C in bar 8

6. Name the lowest note in the piece.
   A (bar 3-4)

Test 10

Look at the following piece then answer the questions below.

1. What does > mean under the notes in bar 7?
   accent the notes

2. Give the Italian words and the English meaning of *mp*.
   mezzo piano   moderately soft

3. How many staccato notes are there in the piece?
   10 (ten)

4. Name in order the rests at the beginning of the piece. ⌣
   dotted minim / *half note*   quaver / *quarter note* rest

6. What does ∧ mean over the note in bar 8?
   strongly accent the note

7. What does ▭◁ mean?
   become gradually louder

8. What is the meaning of Con brio?

   with spirit   with vigour

Book 3 page 61

BOOK 4
PUZZLES

QUIZZES

TESTS

Fun Page

Draw a string for each balloon.

Music is Theory Fun

I drew the 'first' one for you.

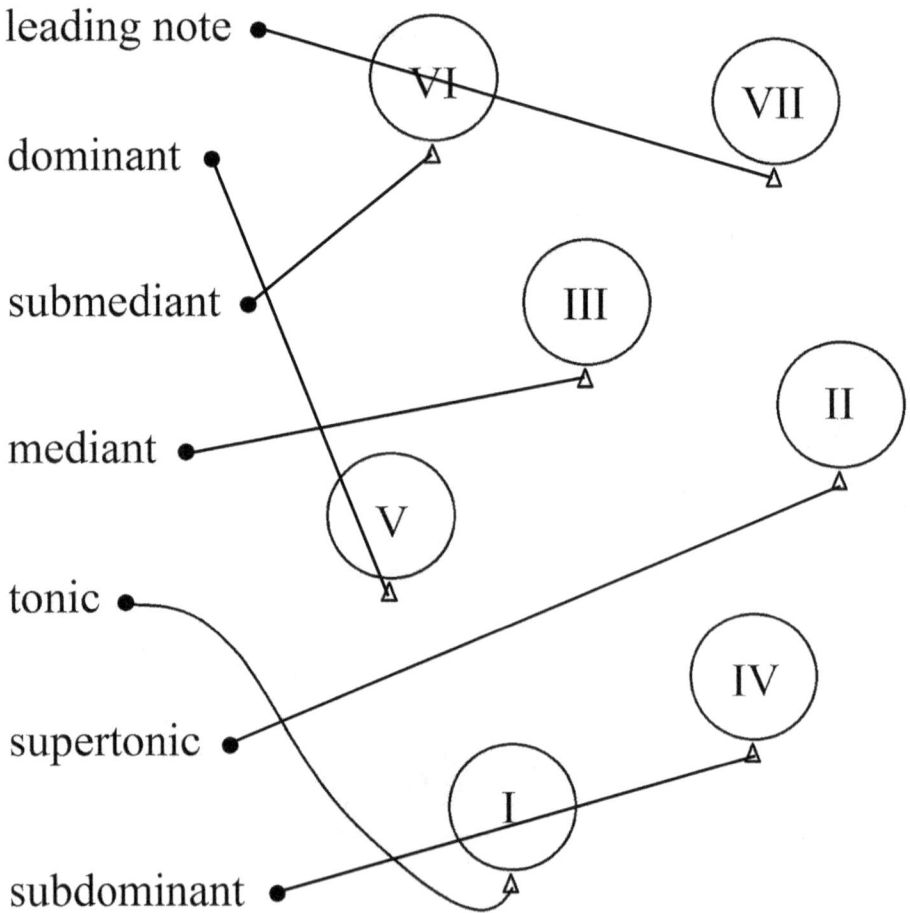

leading note •

VI   VII

dominant •

submediant •   III

                              II

mediant •

        V

tonic •

                    IV

supertonic •

            I

subdominant •

Book 4 page 48

Anagrams

caratacacuci | acciaccatura |

Clue: This ornament is played as quickly as possible on the beat and just before the main note.

ograpige | arpeggio |

Clue: This wavy line means ripple the chord like on a harp.

frecept hofurt | perfect fourth |

Clue: This is an interval of 5 semitones / *5 half steps*.

rajmo veenths | major seventh |

Clue: This is an interval of 11 semitones / *11 half steps*.

hiddinmeis | diminished |

Clue: These intervals are one semitone / *1 half step* less than a minor interval.

tombudanins | subdominant |

Clue: This is also called chord IV.

Crossword

Across

1 hammered out

6 sadly

7 hold back

8 minor key with 4 flats

9 major key with 5 sharps

10 sweetly

13 below

15 sighing

Down

1 mysteriously

2 very

3 slowly

4 animated, lively

5 loud then immediately soft

11 less

12 as if, resembling

14 in the style of

Musical terms word search

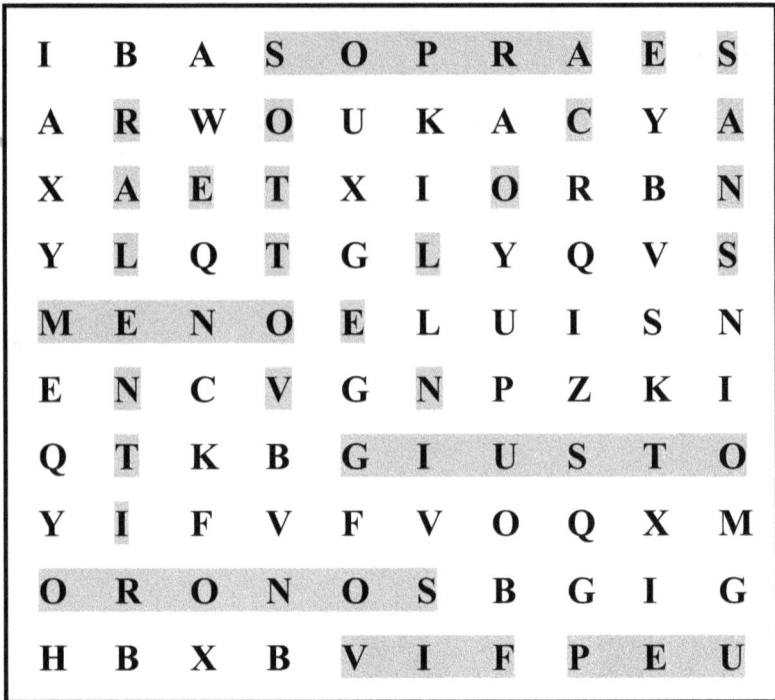

I	B	A	S	O	P	R	A	E	S
A	R	W	O	U	K	A	C	Y	A
X	A	E	T	X	I	O	R	B	N
Y	L	Q	T	G	L	Y	Q	V	S
M	E	N	O	E	L	U	I	S	N
E	N	C	V	G	N	P	Z	K	I
Q	T	K	B	G	I	U	S	T	O
Y	I	F	V	F	V	O	Q	X	M
O	R	O	N	O	S	B	G	I	G
H	B	X	B	V	I	F	P	E	U

Meaning	Musical term
lively	**vif**
slow down	**slow down**
held back	**retenu**
exact, proper	**giusto**
with rich tone	**sonoro**
without	**sans**
above	**sopra**
below	**sotto**
swift	**veloce**
less	**meno**
little	**peu**

Quiz 1

Put a tick / *check mark* (✓) for the correct answer.

1. marcato
- ☐ majestically
- ☐ in a military style
- ☐ hammered out
- ☑ marked, accented

2. sadly
- ☑ dolente
- ☐ dolce
- ☐ dolore
- ☐ delicato

3. with a strong accent
- ☐ forte
- ☐ fortissimo
- ☑ forzando
- ☐ pesante

4. ∾
- ☑ upper turn
- ☐ upper mordent
- ☐ lower mordent
- ☐ shake

5. with vigour
- ☐ con anima
- ☑ con brio
- ☐ con moto
- ☐ con spirito

6. meno
- ☑ less
- ☐ more
- ☐ moderately
- ☐ much

7. from the beginning
- ☐ dal segno
- ☐ a tempo
- ☑ da capo
- ☐ prima volta

8.
- ☐ short, detached
- ☐ accent the note
- ☑ staccatissimo
- ☐ staccato

Quiz 2

Do you know these orchestral instruments? Write in the box the name of the instrument being played.

bassoon	cello

French horn	timpani / kettle drums

Handy hints for tests

This section is for you to practise the different types of questions you could have in a test or an exam.

The questions could be on any topic covered in this book and in Music Theory is Fun Books 1, 2 and 3.

Revise each topic in this book thoroughly.

Don't forget to study musical terms and signs – they are **always** included.

Practice
makes perfect !

Practice
makes perfect !

If you have worked through this book carefully and understood each topic, this will be an easy task for you.

Before you begin any test, write out your key signature chart (see page 7). Always refer to the chart when tackling questions that require you to know a key signature.

Test 1

1. Name this interval.

   major 7th ☐   augmented 6th ☐   diminished 7th ☑

2. Smorzando means

   gradually slower ☐   dying away ☑   tearfully ☐

3. Which minor key has 5 sharps in its key signature?

   F ☐   C ☐   G♯ ☑

4. Which minor key has 4 flats in its key signature?

   F ☑   C ☐   B ☐

5. Which note is the mediant in this minor key?

       G ☐   A ☑   D ☐

6. This note is

   lowered one semitone / *one half step* ☐
   lowered one tone / *one whole step* ☑
   raised one semitone / *one half step* ☐

7. Which is the correct time signature for this bar?

       $\frac{3}{8}$ ☐ $\frac{5}{8}$ ☑ $\frac{5}{4}$ ☐

8. How many semiquavers / *16th notes* are there in this note?

       5 ☐   6 ☐   7 ☑

Book 4 page 56

Test 2

1. Put a Roman numeral under each note in this D major scale.

    I   **II**   **III** **IV**   **V**   **VI** **VII** **VIII**

2. How many quavers / *8th notes* are there in these notes?

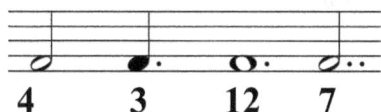

   4   **3**   **12**   **7**

3. Name these ornament signs.

   (a)   **lower mordent**

   (b)   **upper turn**

   (c)   **upper mordent**

   (d) *tr*~~~   **trill or shake**

   (e)   **acciaccatura**

4. What does this metronome setting mean? ♩ **= 80**

   80 crotchet / 80 quarter note beats per minute

5. Write the chromatic scale of G major in the treble clef ascending in semibreves / *whole notes* with key signature.

Test 3

1. Name the four main families of orchestral instruments.

   brass   **percussion**

   strings   **woodwind**

2. What is the meaning of

   (a) sul ponticello   **play near the bridge**

   (b) pizzicato   **plucked**

   (c) arco   **play with the bow**

3. (a) What is the meaning of senza sordini?

   without mute

   (b) Name an instrument that might have this direction.

   any member of the brass or string family

4. Write in semibreves / *whole notes* the scale of D♭ major ascending in the treble clef with key signature.

   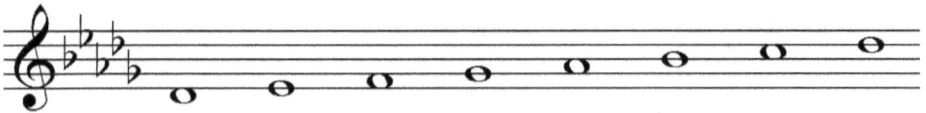

5. Write in semibreves / *whole notes* the scale of G♯ melodic minor descending in the bass clef without key signature.

   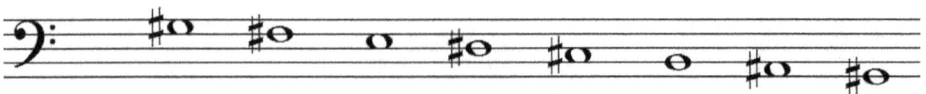

Book 4 page 58

Test 4

1. Write a note above the given note to form the named melodic intervals.

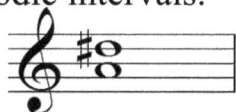

   (a) augmented 4th   (b) diminished 7th.

2. Put accidentals in front of the notes that need them to make the scale of C melodic minor. Do not use a key signature.

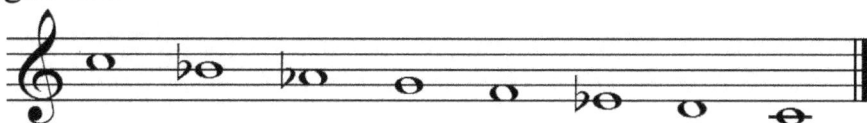

3. Write the scale of G♯ harmonic minor ascending in minims / *half notes* using the bass clef. Do not put a key signature. Add any necessary accidentals.

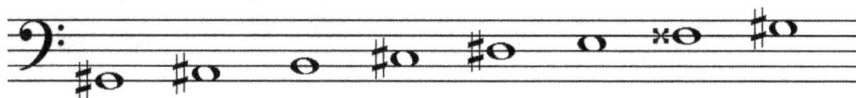

4. **patetico** means

   dying away   ☐
   with feeling   ☑
   tearfully   ☐
   sadly   ☐

5. ♪ is the sign for

   upper mordent   ☐
   appoggiatura   ☐
   acciaccatura   ☑
   trill   ☐

Test 5

1. Name the family for each instrument.

    oboe   **woodwind**

    cello   **strings**

    trumpet   **brass**

    timpani   **percussion**

2. Write the scale of F melodic minor in the bass clef ascending in minims / *half notes* with key signature.

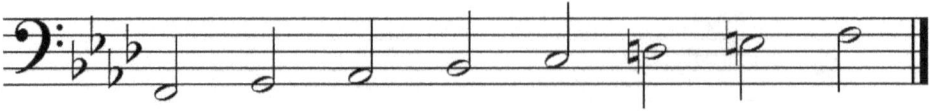

3. Write the letter names of the notes on the white keys.

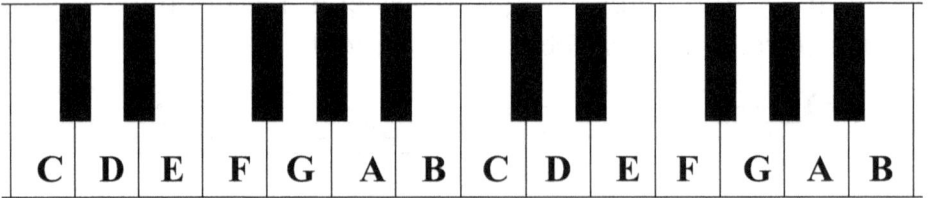

| C | D | E | F | G | A | B | C | D | E | F | G | A | B |

4. Write above the black keys the letter names of (a) the flats and (b) the sharps.

(a) D♭ E♭   G♭ A♭ B♭ (b) C♯ D♯   F♯ G♯ A♯

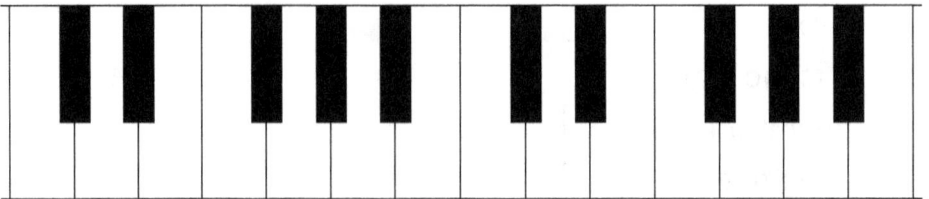

Test 6

1. Write these alto clef notes at the same pitch in the treble clef.

2. Write a chromatic scale beginning on A♭ with key signature ascending in semibreves / *whole notes* using the treble clef. Remember the accidentals.

3. Write a chromatic scale beginning on D without key signature ascending in semibreves / *whole notes* using the alto clef. Put in all necessary accidentals.

4. Describe each of these harmonic intervals fully e.g. major 3rd, perfect 4th.

   perfect 5th   **major 7th**   **major 6th**

5. Name these notes.

   D   **B♭**   **C**

Book 4 page 61

Test 7

1. Find the mistakes in this piece of music and then write it out correctly on the stave below.

2. Write the tonic, subdominant and dominant triads of F major in the treble clef with key signature.

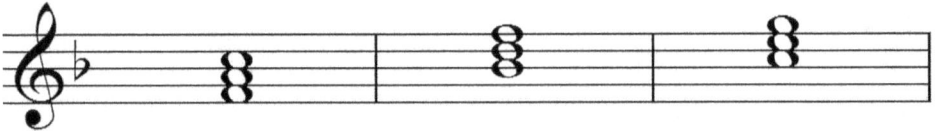

4. Write the tonic, subdominant and dominant triads of F minor in the treble clef with key signature.

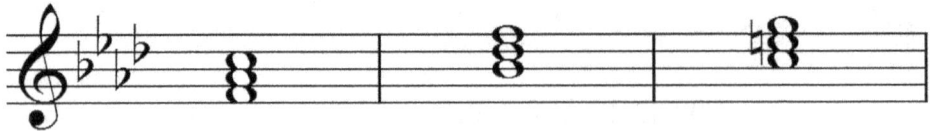

5. Compose rhythms to these words from a poem by Robert Frost.   The woods are lovely, dark and deep
But I have promises to keep
Begin with an anacrusis. Add a time signature.

rhythm	
words	The woods are love-ly, dark and deep, but
rhythm	
words	I have pro - mi - ses to keep.

Test 8

1. Give the meaning of Patetico. **with feeling**

2. Transpose this melody up one octave using the treble clef.

3. Name the notes in bar 3 in order. **D   E♭   C   A**

4. How many demisemiquavers / *32nd notes* is the last note of bar 1 worth? **16**

5. Name two orchestral instruments, one string and one woodwind, that could play this melody so that the pitch sounds the same.
   string **violin**   woodwind **oboe**

6. Which member of the string family usually uses the alto clef? **viola**

7. Tick / *check* the boxes beside two instruments that are not members of the orchestral woodwind family.
   bassoon ☐   tuba ☑   oboe ☐   trombone ☑   flute ☐

Test 9

Look at the following piece of music and answer the questions that follow.

1. Add a key signature in the bass clef and add a time signature in the treble and bass clefs.

2. Copy the treble part in bar 1 and mark the beats with a stroke (|) between each beat.

3. What is the Italian word for the ornament (♪) at the beginning of bar 2 and what does it mean? Is it played quickly or slowly?
   acciaccatura - squeezed in

   played as quickly as possible

4. Give the meaning of ♩ = 120

   120 crotchet / *quarter note* beats in a bar

5. Name the notes in the last chord in the treble clef in bar 2.
   B (natural) G (natural)

6. Name the number and type of interval between the notes in the last chord of bar 2.

   number **6th**   type **minor**

Book 4 page 64

Test 10

Look at this melody and then answer the questions below.

1. Add the time signature of the melody in the correct place.

2. Describe the time signature as simple, compound duple, triple or quadruple. **compound triple**

3. What is the key of the piece? **E♭ major**

4. Give the letter names of the first three notes in bar 1.

   E♭   F   A♭

5. Give the letter name of the highest note in the melody.

   B♭

6. Name the ornaments in bars 3 & 4. **apoggiatura**

7. Look at bar 5 then give the meaning of

   (a) ⁀ **tie the notes**

   (b) 𝆏 **pause on the note**

8. How should the notes in bar 4 be played?

   becoming slower and softer

BOOK 5
PUZZLES

QUIZZES

TESTS

Fun page 1

Add the missing clefs, sharps or flats to show all seven accidentals.

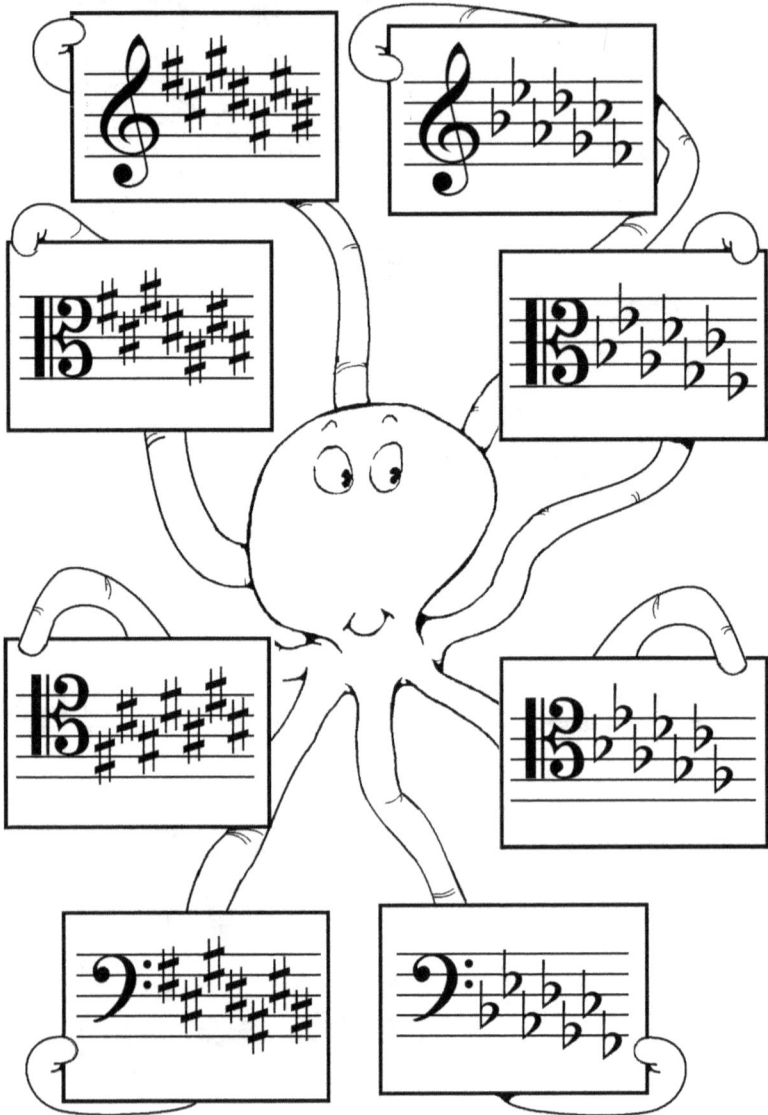

Fun page 2

Tie the balloons to the correct chords in C major.

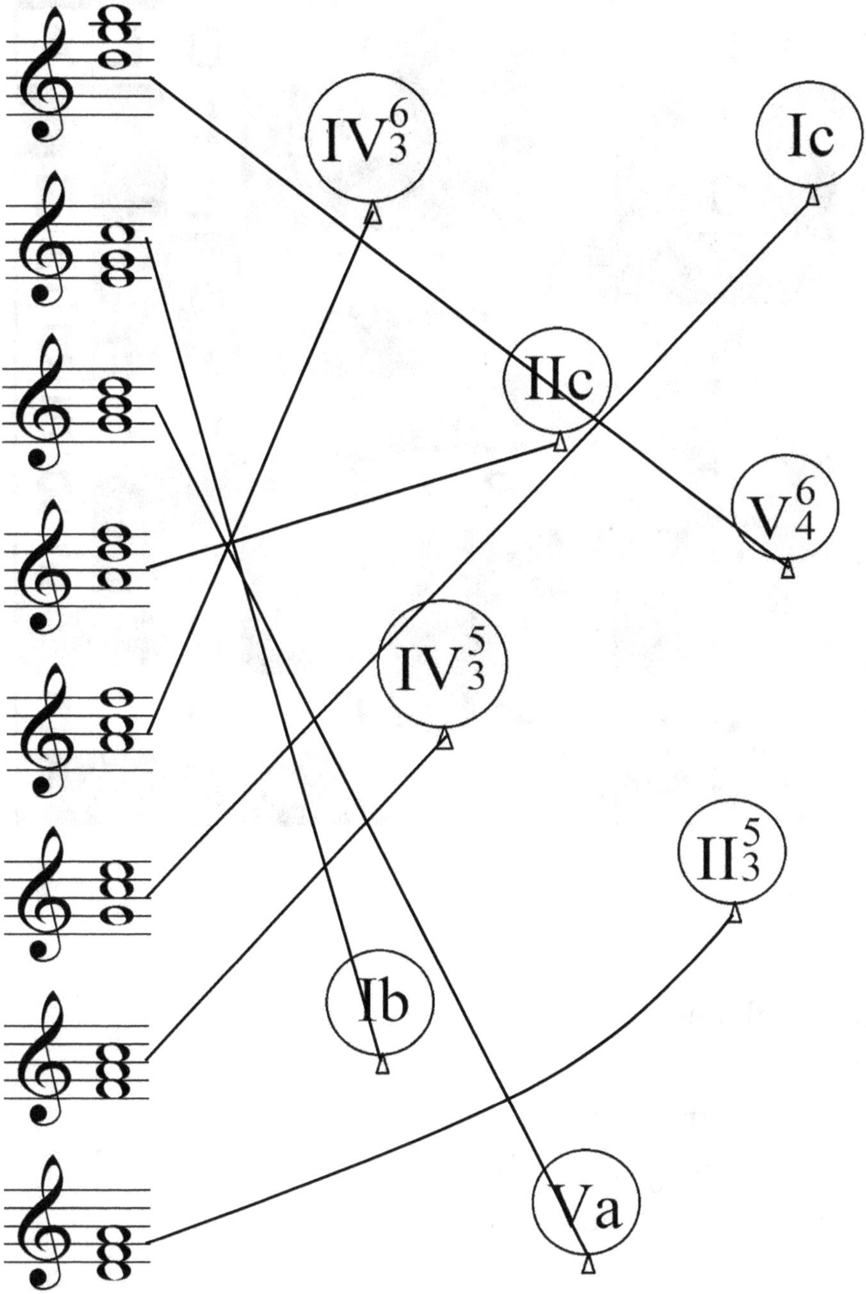

Crossword

Clues

Across

2 minor 7th interval in A minor

4 time

6 stringed instrument with range below violin and above cello

9 woodwind with double reed

10 without

11 note twice the length of a whole note

12 tender, delicate

17 enough, sufficiently

18 woodwind blown across the edge of the hole

19 perfect 5th interval in D major

Down

1 voice below soprano and above tenor

3 full

5 chord 1b in F major

6 turn the page quickly

7 at a moderate speed

8 at a moderate speed

13 clef used for tuba

14 lively

15 unpitched percussion instrument

16 with a strong accent

Musical terms word search

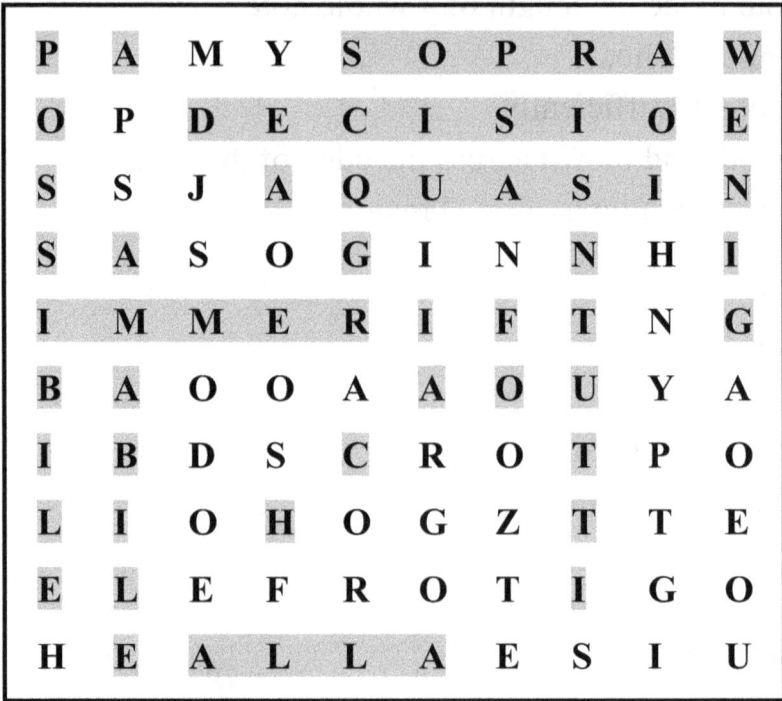

P	A	M	Y	S	O	P	R	A	W
O	P	D	E	C	I	S	I	O	E
S	S	J	A	Q	U	A	S	I	N
S	A	S	O	G	I	N	N	H	I
I	M	M	E	R	I	F	T	N	G
B	A	O	O	A	A	O	U	Y	A
I	B	D	S	C	R	O	T	P	O
L	I	O	H	O	G	Z	T	T	E
E	L	E	F	R	O	T	I	G	O
H	E	A	L	L	A	E	S	I	U

Meaning	Musical term
in the style of	**alla**
slow, leisurely	**adagio**
amiable, pleasant	**amabile**
with determination	**decisio**
simple	**einfach**
always	**immer**
possible	**possibile**
as if, resembling	**quasi**
above	**sopra**
all	**tutti**
little	**wenig**

Anagrams

pemfercit acneced | **imperfect cadence**

Clue: Produced by any chord in front of the dominant.

gallap | **plagal**

Clue: Cadence produced by chord IV followed by chord I.

osnobas | **bassoon**

Clue: Woodwind instrument that uses a double reed.

frits rosenvini | **first inversion**

Clue: Chords such as Ib, IIb, IVb and Vb.

netombro | **trombone**

Clue: Music for this instrument can use tenor or bass clef.

oorspan | **soprano**

Clue: In a short score the part for this voice is on the upper stave.

Quiz 1

Do you know your terms and signs? Tick the correct box.

1. sospirando

☑ sighing

☐ gradually faster

☐ gradually slower

☐ in a speaking manner

2. at a moderate speed

☑ mässig

☐ ruhig

☐ traurig

☐ wenig

3. inverted turn

☐ ♦♦

☐ ∾

☐ ♦♦

☑ ∾

4. with

☐ ohne

☐ sans

☐ senza

☑ avec

5. sempre

☐ above

☑ always

☐ simple

☐ below

6. staccatissimo

☐

☐

☑

☐

Quiz 2

Do you know your orchestral instruments?

Which one has the most strings?

harp

Which one is struck with a mallet?

tubular bells

Which brass instrument has no valves?

trombone

Which woodwind plays the highest note?

piccolo

Which woodwind plays the lowest note?

double bassoon

Which single reed instrument is found mainly in jazz bands?

saxophone

Which is the smallest percussion instrument that is struck and shaken?

tambourine

Which percussion instrument has two sets of wooden bars arranged like piano keys?

xylophone

Handy hints for tests

This section is for you to practise the different types of questions you could have in a test or an exam.

The questions could be on any topic covered in this book and in Music Theory is Fun Books 1 2, 3 and 4.

Revise each topic in this book thoroughly.

Don't forget to study musical terms and signs – they are **always** included.

Practice
makes perfect !

Practice
makes perfect !

If you have worked through this book carefully and understood each topic, this will be an easy task for you.

Before you begin any test, write out your key signature charts (see page 7). Always refer to the charts when tackling questions that require you to know a key signature.

Test 1

1. Name these notes

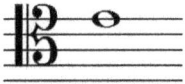

F ☐   D ☐   E ☑

E♭ ☑   B♭ ☐   A ☐

2. Which is the correct time signature?

$\frac{6}{8}$ ☐ $\frac{3}{4}$ ☑ $\frac{3}{8}$ ☐

3. Which rest or rests should complete the bar?

𝄾𝄾 ☑   𝄽 ☐   𝄾. ☐

4. Which note is the dominant of the minor key shown by this key signature?

C♯ ☐   E ☐   D♯ ☑

5. Which note is the subdominant of the minor key shown by this key signature?

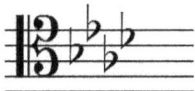

E♭ ☐   C ☐   B♭ ☑

6. Which Roman numeral fits below this dominant chord?

Vb ☐   V ☐   Vc ☑

Test 2

1. Write a one octave C♯ melodic minor scale ascending in minims / *half notes* with key signature in the bass clef.

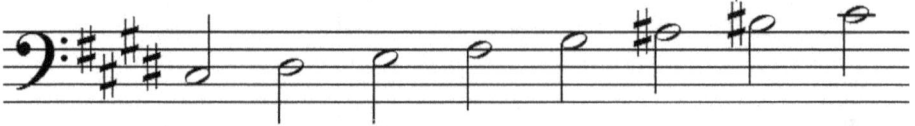

2. Write a one octave E♭ harmonic minor scale in semibreves / *whole notes* descending in the tenor clef without key signature.

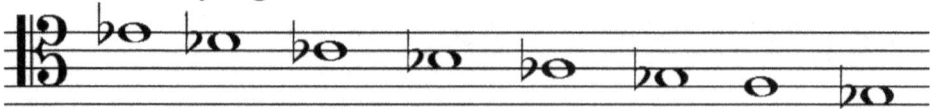

3. Write a one octave chromatic scale of D major with key signature ascending in crotchets / *quarter notes* using the treble clef. Remember to put in the accidentals.

4. Write a rhythm to fit the following words from William Wordsworth's poem *Daffodils*. Give the time signature.

Be - side the   lake,   be - neath the   trees

Flut-ter - ing and   dan - cing in   the   breeze

5. Write a note above the given note to produce the interval.

major 7th   augmented 5th   diminished 6th   minor 3rd

Test 3

1. Write the key signature of 4 flats and one octave ascending of the harmonic minor scale with that key signature. Use semibreves / *whole notes*.

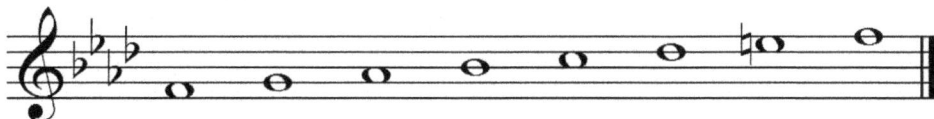

2. Write the scale of E major descending without key signature in semibreves / *whole notes*. Put accidentals in front of the notes as needed.

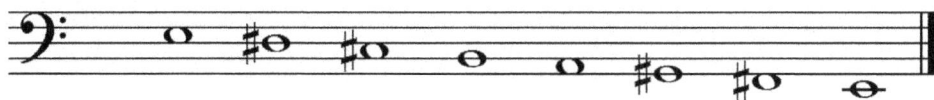

3. Write the tonic, supertonic and dominant triads of C major in root position. Add their Roman numerals.

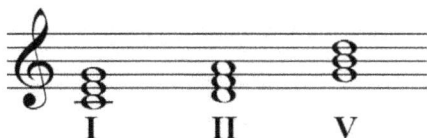

I   II   V

4. Write the tonic, subdominant and dominant triads of D major in their second inversions with the key signature. Add their Roman numerals.

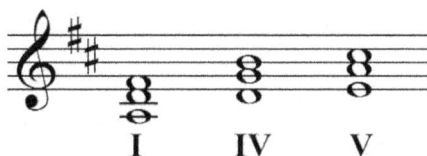

I   IV   V

5. Write the supertonic, subdominant and dominant triads of F major in their first inversions without key signature. Add their Roman numerals and any necessary accidentals.

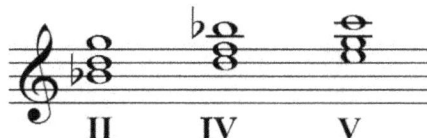

II   IV   V

Test 4

1. Write the following notes at the same pitch but using the given clef.

2. Transpose this melody up a perfect 5th in each of these clefs. Use a key signature.

3. Using crotchets / *quarter notes*, write out 4-part chords for SATB in short score using the chords shown by the Roman numerals.

(G minor) Vc   (E major) IVb

Test 5

1. Write this melody a perfect 5th **lower** in each of the given clefs. Include the time signature and new key signature.

2. Write the following notes at the same pitch but using the given clef.

3. Using semibreves / *whole notes*, write out 4-part chords for SATB in short score using the chords shown by the Roman numerals.

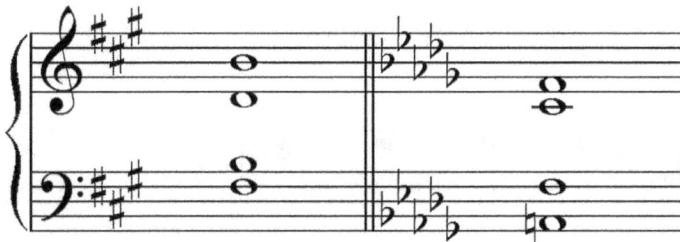

(A major) IIc   (B♭ minor) Vb

Book 5 page 73

Test 6

1. Put a time signature for each bar / *measure* of notes.

2. Rewrite this passage, doubling the time values. Add the new time signature.

3. Write one bar / *measure* in quavers / *8th notes* using the given time signature. Place the notes on the line or in the space for E.

(a)

(b)

(c)

(d)

Book 5 page 74

Test 7

1. Describe fully each of these melodic intervals, e.g. minor 3rd, perfect 4th.

(a)

perfect 5th

(b)

major 6th

(c)

major 7th

(d)

major 3rd

2. Write a higher note to form the named melodic interval with the given note.

 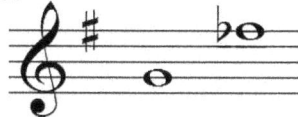 

perfect 5th   diminished 7th   augmented 5th

3. Rewrite this passage in the alto clef

4. Give the letter names of the strings of the viola.

C   G   D   A

Test 8

1. This rhythm begins on the first beat of the bar. Put in the missing bar lines.

2. Names this cadence.

plagal cadence in D minor ☐

perfect cadence in F major ☑

imperfect cadence in F minor ☐

3. Fill in the missing words.

a) In a perfect cadence the **dominant chord** leads to

the **tonic chord**.

b) The subdominant chord plus the tonic chord

is a **plagal** cadence.

4. Fill in the Roman numerals.

a) A plagal cadence = **IV** + **I**

b) A perfect cadence = **V** + **I**

5. Tick the box for the ornament that should be played as shown.

tr 〰〰 ☐   ⋀⋀ ☐   ⫯⋀ ☑

Test 9

After looking at this extract, answer the questions below.

1. Name the ornament (♪) in bar 2. **appoggiatura**

2. Name the ornament (⪩⪩) in bar 4. **upper mordent**

3. Give the meaning of leggiero.
   lightly

4. How should you play the notes of the 3rd beat in bar 1?
   semi staccato

5. What does the sign mean over the note in bar 5?
   pause on the note

6. Give the meaning of *pp*.
   very soft

7. Complete bar 6 with a rest or rests.

8. Name all the notes in bar 4 in order.

   A   F♯   D   F♯   D   G

9. Give the meaning of
   (a) *mp*   **moderately soft**
   (b) ▭▭▭▭   **becoming softer**

Test 10

Allegretto

1. Name the highest note in this piece of music. **D**

2. In which key is this piece? **D major**

3. Give the meaning of
   allegretto **slightly slower than allegro**

   sfz   **with sudden accent**

4. What is the name of the ornament (♪) in bar 4?

   acciaccatura

5. How should you play the last four notes in bar 6?
   legato / smoothly

6. Which note is played the loudest? note: **D** in bar **9**

7. What does ⟨< mean?   **gradually louder**

8. How should the three notes in bar 7 be played?
   held on and given their full value

9. What should you do when playing this piece and you reach
   the end of bar 8?

   repeat starting at bar 5

10. How many times should you play bar 9? **once**

www.ingramcontent.com/pod-product-compliance
Lightning Source LLC
Chambersburg PA
CBHW070524030426
42337CB00016B/2096